A FIRST LOOK AT AMERICA'S PRESIDENTS

HARRY S. TRUMAN

The 33rd President

by Kevin Blake

Consultant: David Greenberg, Professor of History
Rutgers University
New Brunswick, New Jersey

BEARPORT PUBLISHING

New York, New York

Credits

Cover, Courtesy Harry S. Truman Library; 4, Courtesy Harry S. Truman Library; 5, Portrait by Leo S. Stern/Courtesy Harry S. Truman Library; 6L, © Kornienko/Dreamstime; 6R, Hare Studios of Independence, Missouri/Courtesy Harry S. Truman Library; 7, © Shaday35/Dreamstime; 9L, Courtesy Harry S. Truman Library; 9R, Courtesy Harry S. Truman Library; 10, Courtesy Harry S. Truman Library; 11, © AP Photo/stf; 12, Courtesy U.S. Army; 13T, Courtesy Harry S. Truman Library; 13B, Courtesy U.S. Navy/Victor Jorgensen; 14, © Everett Historical/Shutterstock; 15, Courtesy Harry S. Truman Library; 16, Courtesy Harry S. Truman Library; 17, Courtesy U.S. Army; 18–19, National Archives; 22, © GNagel/Dreamstime; 23B, © Leo Bruce Hemphill/Dreamstime; 24, catwalker/Shutterstock.

Publisher: Kenn Goin
Senior Editor: Joyce Tavolacci
Creative Director: Spencer Brinker
Production and Photo Research: Shoreline Publishing Group LLC

Library of Congress Cataloging-in-Publication Data

Blake, Kevin, 1978– author.
  Harry S. Truman : the 33rd president / by Kevin Blake.
     pages cm. — (A first look at America's presidents)
  Includes bibliographical references and index.
  Audience: Age 4–8.
  ISBN 978-1-943553-29-7 (library binding) — ISBN 1-943553-29-7 (library binding)
  1. Truman, Harry S., 1884-1972—Juvenile literature. 2. Presidents—United States—Biography—Juvenile literature.
3. United States—Politics and government—1945-1953—Juvenile literature. I. Title.
  E814.B57 2016
  973.918092—dc23
  [B]
                                    2015033038

For more information, write to Bearport Publishing Company, Inc., 45 West 21st Street, Suite 3B, New York, New York 10010. Printed in the United States of America.

10 9 8 7 6 5 4 3 2 1

CONTENTS

Man of the People 4

Little Reader 6

College Dreams 8

Senator from Missouri 10

A Sudden President 12

A Helping Hand 14

The Cold War 16

Remembering Truman 18

Timeline 20

Facts and Quotes 22

Glossary 23

Index 24

Read More 24

Learn More Online 24

About the Author 24

Man of the People

Harry S. Truman faced many challenges during his life. He had to work hard to get ahead. Along the way, he learned to be honest, tough, and caring. As president, he made hard decisions to help Americans.

President Truman meets with a group of young farmers.

Harry S. Truman was the 33rd president. He served from 1945 to 1953.

Little Reader

Harry S. Truman was born in 1884 in Missouri. He grew up in a small town. As a child, he liked to play the piano. He also loved to read. In fact, he read every book in the town's library!

Harry had trouble seeing and wore glasses.

A house in Independence, Missouri, where Harry once lived

Harry's middle name is just the letter S. The S honors his grandfathers, who both had S in their names.

7

College Dreams

After high school, Truman wanted to go to college but couldn't afford to. In 1917, he joined the army. He fought bravely during World War I (1914–1918). When he came back home, Truman ran a clothing store in Missouri with an army buddy.

A poster from World War I asking young men to join the U.S. Army

8

In 1919, Harry Truman married Bess Wallace. The two met when they were six years old.

Harry Truman and Bess Wallace on their wedding day

Truman in his army uniform during World War I

Senator from Missouri

People from Missouri saw that Truman was smart and honest. They chose him to become a judge. He did such a good job that they **elected** him to the U.S. Senate. Soon, even President Franklin D. Roosevelt noticed him. He asked Truman to run for vice president in 1944.

From 1939 to 1945, the United States fought Japan and other countries in World War II.

Senator Truman became famous for cutting government spending during World War II.

REGISTER AND VOTE
DEMOCRATIC

ROOSEVELT   TRUMAN
FOR LASTING PEACE ★ SECURITY FOR ALL

Roosevelt and
Truman won the
1944 election.

A Sudden President

In April 1945, President Roosevelt died. As a result, Truman became president. He had a lot of tough decisions to make. Many Americans were being killed fighting in World War II. President Truman ordered two **atomic bombs** to be dropped on Japan. He knew this would end the war—and it did.

The atomic bomb blast over Nagasaki, Japan

More than 60 million people died during World War II.

Truman being sworn in as president after the death of President Roosevelt

Americans celebrate the end of World War II.

13

A Helping Hand

Many European countries were in ruins after World War II. Truman sent money so they could rebuild.

Truman also helped people at home. He improved health care for the poor. He also ended **segregation** in the Army and Navy. This let black and white Americans serve together.

A European city destroyed after World War II

In 1948, Truman was elected to another four years as president.

Few thought that Truman would win the 1948 election. One newspaper printed that Truman had lost. Oops!

The Cold War

After World War II, the **Soviet Union** tried to take over other countries. This period was called the Cold War. Truman wanted to help America's friends. He sent food to the German people. He also sent American soldiers to help South Korea fight Soviet **allies**.

Truman wanted countries to solve their problems peacefully. So he helped create the United Nations in 1945.

Truman sent
soldiers to try to
help South Korea.

Remembering Truman

Truman helped the United States become a better country. Many of his ideas, such as health care for the poor, were made into laws. He also put an end to World War II. Many people consider Truman to be one of our greatest presidents.

After leaving the White House, Truman moved back to Missouri. He died in 1972. He was 88 years old.

After Truman left office, he continued working to improve health care. In 1965, he looked on as President Lyndon Johnson signed a new health care law.

Truman

TIMELINE

Here are some major events from Harry S. Truman's life.

1884
Harry S. Truman is born in Lamar, Missouri.

1901
Truman graduates from high school.

1919
Truman marries Bess Wallace.

1880 1890 1900 1910 1920

1917
Truman enters the army and fights in France during World War I (1914–1918).

1944

Truman is elected
vice president
under President
Franklin Roosevelt.

1934

Truman becomes
a U.S. Senator.

1948

Truman is elected
to a second term
as president.

1930   1940   1950   1960   1970

1926

Truman is chosen
to be a judge in
Jackson County,
Missouri.

1945

President
Roosevelt
dies. Truman
becomes
president.

1972

Truman dies
in Kansas City,
Missouri.

The University of Missouri's mascot is named after Harry Truman. It's called Truman the Tiger.

"You know that being an American is more than a matter of where your parents came from. It is a belief that all men are created free and equal and that everyone deserves an even break."

When he became president after Roosevelt's death, Truman told reporters: "I felt like the moon, the stars, and all the planets had fallen on me."

Harry and Bess had one daughter, named Margaret.

HARRY S. TRUMAN

1884 - 1972

Born in Lamar. 33rd U.S. President (1945 - 1953)
Considered one of the nation's greatest presidents
and most remarkable statesman.

Presented by Speaker Bob F. Griffin
from Speaker's Annual Golf Classic Donations.

William J. Williams, Sculptor

"The buck stops here."

22

GLOSSARY

allies (AL-eyez) people or nations that work together for a common cause

atomic bombs (uh-TOM-ik BOMZ) very powerful bombs that can destroy entire cities

elected (ih-LEK-tud) chosen by the people through a vote

segregation (seg-ruh-GAY-shun) keeping people of different races apart

Soviet Union (SOH-vee-uht YOON-yuhn) a former country that was centered around Russia

United Nations (yoo-NYE-tid NAY-shuhnz) an organization that helps different countries come together to solve problems

Index

atomic bomb 12
childhood 6–7
Cold War 16
education 8, 20
elections 10–11, 15, 21
health care 14, 18–19
Japan 10, 12

Missouri 6–7, 10, 18, 21, 22
Roosevelt, Franklin D. 10–11, 12, 21
segregation 14
South Korea 16–17
Soviet Union 16

United Nations 16
U.S. Senate 10, 21
vice president 10–11, 21
Wallace, Bess 9, 20, 22
World War I 8–9, 20
World War II 10, 12–13, 14, 18

Read More

Elston, Heidi M.D. *Harry S. Truman: 33rd President of the United States (United States Presidents).* Edina, MN: ABDO (2009).

Gaines, Anne Graham. *Harry S. Truman: Our Thirty-Third President (Presidents of the U.S.A.).* North Mankato, MN: The Child's World (2009).

Gregory, Josh. *Franklin D. Roosevelt: The 32nd President (A First Look at America's Presidents).* New York: Bearport (2015).

Learn More Online

To learn more about Harry S. Truman, visit
www.bearportpublishing.com/AmericasPresidents

Truman announces Japan's surrender, Aug. 14, 1945

About the Author: Kevin Blake writes books for kids. This is his eleventh title. He lives in Providence, Rhode Island, with his wife, Melissa, and their son, Sam.